Mass Education

A Concise Guide to Catholic Liturgy

Dear Aunt Judy,
I hope reading this
brings you as much
joy as writing it did
for me!
Love you,
Adam Thomé

By Adam Thomé

With a Foreword by Timothy Ferreira

DEDICATION

This book is dedicated to all who ever asked 'Why should I bother?' when considering going to Mass, and to my dear Analia and Miguel for helping me see the answer.

CONTENTS

FOREWORD

As the son of an ordained Roman Catholic deacon, it's safe
to say that I basically grew up in the Church. I always lived
near the church; received my education at the church's
parish school; attended Mass at the church every week with
my class and then again with my family on the weekend;
and received the sacraments in the church. Over the course
of my formative years, that's a lot of churchiness. So it
came as something of a surprise to me when I started
reading Adam Thomé's "Mass Education" series of articles
(published by Catholic Majority on its website) and found
out that I didn't know the slightest thing about the liturgy I
had been a part of for decades.

I've always been drawn to the Mass for its pomp and
grandeur, its flashiness and drama — some call this the
Church's "smells and bells." When I got to be an older
teenager in high school (and later, in college), I got a bad
case of intellectual snobbishness. My rebellion took the
form of effectively leaving the Church, and having few kind
things to say about it when asked. Such is the common

adolescent experience of Our People. Since I studied philosophy and obtained my bachelor degree in philosophy, there was a fundamental part of me that had not given up the quest for truth, for Source. In the process, I never looked back, and that was ultimately what took me so long to return to the Church.

At some point after college, I belatedly discovered that much of what we know about the Church comes from a society that is either openly hostile to or perilously ignorant of Her. It was at this point that I looked back and discovered to my amazement (and relief) that what the Church had to offer was what had been missing from my life since childhood: meaning, community, and peace. I made it a point to read all that I could about Church history, including important and formative documents like the papal encyclicals and apostolic exhortations, hagiographies, devotionals, and the documents prepared at the Second Vatican Council. I devoured the *Catechism of the Catholic Church* in just a few sittings, returning to it frequently for nourishment or clarity. It was only after this preliminary research that I set my alarm to wake me on a Sunday morning and made my way to my local parish.

When I arrived at the church, the only thing that surprised me after all these years was how well-attended the Mass was. Movies so often depict a priest preaching (poorly) to near-empty pews. I expected something similar. And at any rate, I live south of the Mason-Dixon line. I didn't even know there were other Catholics in my community, let alone enough to completely fill the pews. Other than that, everything was the same. The Mass followed the same formula that I had grown up with and apparently stored in my long-term memory. The words came back to me like I had never been gone. More importantly, I was treated as though I had never been gone.

I was just another member of the community. I found that I could not only "say my lines," but I could anticipate and silently parrot the lines of the priest. We were still praying for "John Paul, our pope." The only other "new" thing I learned was the name of our local bishop: Joseph. That was easy enough to remember. By the end of Mass, it seemed like it had been an otherworldly experience — like the previous decade had never occurred. I was back. And I was an automaton.

Then came November 2011. Although there had been plenty of warning, the changes in the Liturgy still seemed sudden, even rushed. What had been a lovely congregation of people robotically "saying their lines" and "doing their moves" became an awkward congregation of people doing and saying, it seemed to me, whatever they wanted. There were those who had done their homework and proudly displayed their acumen at incorporating liturgical change. Then there were those who got everything "right," but it seemed like they were on a tape delay. They spoke haltingly, unsure of themselves, moving only after everyone else moved, and clutching their preparatory documents like they needed it to live and breathe. A few members of the congregation took a more oppositional tone, proudly reciting the "old lines," and basically running interference in an effort to make the changes go away through their own obstinance and sheer will. The remainder of the congregation, myself included, tried our best, often mumbling and stumbling as our brains rewired themselves. Although the changes were relatively minor, it wasn't pretty out of the gate, and it started to feel like a fractured community.

Since I was born post-Vatican II, I had never experienced this feeling of disorganization and disunity during a Mass. It was troubling, and it made me uncomfortable. It wasn't that I couldn't get behind the changes — that was over and done. What made me uncomfortable was how difficult such small changes proved to be. If we had been automatons before, we were short-circuiting now. What did this say about us? For me, it meant that for more than thirty years, I had "recited" the Liturgy, and never "participated in" the Liturgy.

The experience of Mass has improved immensely since Advent of 2011, to the point where I can report that we're essentially back to normal. (Well, except for during the holidays when the returning Catholics, who've managed to miss the memo about the liturgical changes, come to Mass. All the same, it's good to see them.) Regardless of how smoothly Mass goes now, the disorienting experience of feeling out of place when the changes were made stuck with me. My stumbling over the changes caused me to question my own sincerity. So when Catholic Majority launched its website and began publishing the "Mass Education" series of articles by Adam Thomé, I read them with great interest.

After the first few of Adam's articles were posted, I approached him with the idea of turning the series into a book to make his insights and explanations more accessible outside the purview of the website. Thankfully, he was amenable to the idea, and now here we are. I hope that you will enjoy these articles — now chapters — as much as I have. I know that you will never experience the Liturgy in the same way again.

As a fellow staff contributor to Catholic Majority, I have the privilege of speaking with Adam on a fairly regular basis. His appreciation and love for the Liturgy is palpable and it comes through in this book. I also know that Adam is a font of knowledge and wisdom, and that this book is just the tip of the iceberg. I look forward to rereading *Mass*

Education, and hope that this is just the beginning of a long and fruitful lifetime of elucidating the mysterious and the obscure.

Although I grew up in the Church, *Mass Education* taught me what I had never learned, and it does so in a way that is both simple and beautiful. I pray that this book might come into your life at the right time, as it did for me, and that through it, you will come to a fuller appreciation of the Liturgy, and ultimately a fuller spiritual life.

Timothy Ferreira
Staff Contributor, Catholic Majority
Wake Forest, North Carolina

1

INTRODUCTION

A PERFECT SONG OF PRAISE AND THANKSGIVING

I can remember sitting through music theory classes and painstakingly analyzing and questioning each and every individual note of a Bach choral. We would spend a whole class period talking about how an arrangement of four notes in one beat of one measure could completely change the entire character of the piece, taking the composition in a completely different sonic direction. When we pulled our ears away from the microscope and again conceived of the whole, the experience of the music was enriched and deepened. A new level of awareness entered us.

These chapters will be devoted to dissecting the celebration of the Mass into its various parts, and analyzing the individual components one by one. With a historical, theological, and spiritual eye, we will look at the parts of the Mass and how they are intricately woven into that *"one perfect sacrifice, through which God sanctifies the world in Christ."* Through our knowledge of the parts, we will then be able to step back and see how the whole may be conceived of as a tapestry woven by Christ's grace and salvation, through whom beauty flows forth in the lives we live.

Through our careful examination, the Mass — a perfect symphony of varying movements, whose notes and dynamics sing the perfect song of praise and thanksgiving — will transcend obligation and become an indispensable source of spiritual vitality, through the Presence in the Eucharist. Thus, the Eucharist, being the source and summit of our faith and identity, becomes the climactic moment (but not the end!) of our Eucharistic celebration as this symphony transforms us to be that song sung unto the world outside of the church gates. We will examine how these notes harmonize with each other, and their compositional interdependency, so that our active presence within Liturgy denies passivity in our coming to Mass, and we can then truly become resounding instruments of peace.

In the next chapter, we look at the entrance procession, beginning from the time we make the decision to come to Mass and continuing until the priest ascends the altar, as we foster unity and introduce our thoughts to the mystery we are about to celebrate…

And so we begin.

2

THE ENTRANCE

There are basically four purposes for the entrance, each encapsulating one aspect of its role as part of the Introductory Rites of the Mass:

1. To open the celebration;
2. To accompany the procession of the ministers and clergy;
3. To foster unity among the gathered; and
4. To introduce thoughts to the mystery.

The Entrance happens long before these functionary acts. Before we even arrive in the parking lot, we voluntarily make a decision to come to Mass. And even before that decision was made, we experienced the impulse to attend. This original impulse is worth consideration. Granted, years of obligatory attendance might seem more entrenched habit than a weekly Deistic impulse, but fortunately, our minds are such that we have mental access to further tracing, going further down the faith family lines until we find ourselves in the upper room with Jesus himself and hear firsthand the command to "do this in memory of me." So let us take it as a given that we have been called to attend and actively participate in Mass, and that we have answered in the affirmative.

Let's look at the four purposes of the entrance. Numbers (1) and (2) are fairly pragmatic: the entrance opens the celebration and accompanies the procession of the people. The remaining functions, however, offer a window into the mystery: the fostering of unity and the introducing of our thoughts to the mystery of the Mass.

The fostering of unity happens on various levels of awareness. The very tactile sense that we all sit in close proximity, in a Church, and in pews next to family, friends, and strangers creates unity in an undeniably real spatial sense. On a larger macro level, the reality that we have gathered on the same day to celebrate the same mysteries worldwide with the universal Church creates unity on a global level. Further, when we sing (and listen) together, we experience, on a quantum-physical level, a physical and vibratory unity. This is a mathematical (and perhaps spiritual) reality. Metaphysically speaking, the text sung becomes a communal and musical profession, sung by individuals momentarily transcending their individualities, creating a unified sense of oneness, united in faith and belief (or desired faith and belief), which then invites us into mystery.

The introducing of thoughts to the mystery is unifying in and of itself: the unifying agent being Jesus Christ. The Liturgy's desire for unity of thoughts to mystery assumes a diversity of hearts and minds (in a more observational then negative sense) but yet in a greater sense that simply offers unity in Christ's salvific work and the mystery of faith in the Eucharist as the most perfect paradigm of unity.

Mysteries, by their nature, foster meditation. A mystery assumes an unknown, or a not-yet-fully-grasped, and our dwelling upon that mystery, both as individuals and as a community, brings us out of *now* and into contact with the *realm of the infinite*, and into Christ whose love is beyond the confines of time and space. This is indeed mysterious and worthy of a prayerful meditation. In this unified alignment with Christ, sanctifying grace can and will abundantly flow.

So, this is the entrance. We have entered. In the next chapter, we continue to look at the Mass and explore the reverencing and ascent of the altar and the signs and symbols inherent within this act.

3

THE GREETING OF THE ALTAR AND THE PEOPLE

So, we have entered the Church. Now we continue to look at the Introductory Rites to the Mass and explore the reverencing and ascent of the altar, and the signs and symbols inherent in this particular act.

The Liturgical procession reaches the steps of the altar, and makes what is called a profound bow out of reverence. Currently, there is a distinction between a *head bow* and a *full body bow*, the latter being made before the altar and at certain times throughout the Mass.

Let's look at the bow itself. The bow signals a profound sign of respect, a humbling, or a lowering of one's self before a person or a representative sign or symbol. Bowing originated as a remnant gesture of antiquity from the times of socially accepted slavery, and the bowing before one's master. Over time, the servility aspect of bowing organically developed into a sign of politeness, greeting, reverence, and respect — a gesture conspicuous in all major world religions and their religious rites. In this, we bow before Christ and His altar, in reverence and in gratitude for His sacrifice upon the cross, a sacrifice which was arguably the most profound and humbling of all bows.

The priest and deacon then ascend the altar and reverence again, this time with a kiss. The kiss, like the bow, has its origins from ancient cultures, deriving from the belief that to unite lips was to unite souls with breath (which was believed to contain the souls). The etymological relation between "Spirit" and "breath" confirms this. The evolution of the kiss retained its unifying characteristics, but also became a sign of reverence and greeting both in secular and sacred realms. The kissing of the altar could then be seen as a unifying of the priest with Christ, who is present in the sacrifice of the altar, and made present in the people gathered.

Once the entrance chant or song is concluded, the priest, together with the people, then opens with the sign of the cross, a communal profession in the sacrifice of the cross, and its centrality in Trinitarian belief. With the gesture of tracing the cross, we physically unite the mind (Father) to the heart (Son), and invoke the guidance of the Holy Spirit (shoulders). It publicly displays not only our belief, but also our desire to unite ourselves to living in the way of Christ and to make the actions and thoughts of our lives an act of thanksgiving and gratitude for his saving deed.

In an acknowledgement of a now present reality, the priest greets the people saying that the Lord is with them, which the people reciprocate with acknowledgement of the Lord's presence within him. Having united into this mystery of presence, and with hearts and minds now joined by the Spirit's grace, preparations are now made to become more fully receptive as a people and as individuals to the graces offered. At this point, we begin the penitential rite, which we will discuss next.

4

THE PENITENTIAL RITE

Let us call to mind our sins…

One of our first participatory acts during the Mass occurs when we call to mind our sinfulness, and ask forgiveness of our sins. The *Confiteor*, the first option for the penitential rite, captures the essence of this rite, and the beauty of mercy.

I confess… I take ownership of my words and deeds and bring them to present awareness, claiming my actions and thoughts as deriving from my own free will, assigning no blame.

…to almighty God… A confession before God whose presence has been both externally and internally acknowledged as being within the gathered people. We make a confession that is received in the instant of our speaking it.

…and to you my brothers and sisters… Humbling,

yet unifying, as not only do we confess to, but also receive confession from, those with whom we live and walk our Christian lives in this penitential rite. For a moment, we become both confessee and confessor.

...that I have greatly sinned... (formerly: *...that I have sinned through my own fault...*) Admission that where several options were presented, one less than love was chosen, and blame may be assigned nowhere except within. Other choices could have been made, but a lesser, destructive, unloving choice was made instead. Fault acknowledges an inextricable link between doer and action.

...through my faults, through my faults, through my most grievous faults... At first the idea of striking the breast three times with each utterance seemed to me to be strangely self-mortifying, and I felt very uncomfortable doing so. As I went through this motion though, I began to imagine this 'strike' as a loving pat, from Christ, done with the intention of encouraging me with something like, *"your heart, your heart, your heart I will renew."*

...in my thoughts... The very important aspect and reality that thoughts have to impress upon the world and those around us. No thought exists without consequence and no thought is benign.

...in my words... Begotten from thoughts, words contain a different, perhaps deeper impact. No less real, words, from a theological vantage point, may either be constructive or destructive to the degree that they reflect the mission of Christ.

...in what I have done... Thoughts beget words and actions, and thoughts not born of love and a Christ-centered disposition will not further the realization of the kingdom, but will prevent this realization. Not only by what is done, but

...what I have failed to do... Inactivity, despite its absence of anything observable, is still action.

...Therefore I ask... To ask is a statement of invitation, an invitation to open a line of communication, verbal or non-verbal, so as to realize communion with another.

...Blessed Mary, ever virgin, with all the angels and saints... No one lives in this world alone and no one lives in this world without a connection to something greater than him or herself, something "other worldly." This is a plea to a higher reality, a level of blessedness ascended to by saints, with whom we seek communion, and who have gone before us.

...and to you my brothers and sisters... Again, we are not alone and the more 'one' we can conceive of ourselves to be, the more perfectly we will come to realize our oneness in the Lord. This is also not only a oneness with the saints, but with those called to be saints with us here on earth.

...to pray for me... As we ask for prayer, we are being asked to pray at the same time. If all of us prayed for each other, all would be prayed for, and we would experience a communal lifting, a sort of ascension where we transcend individual frailty to know a corporate sanctification, and an empowering and emboldening to truly live the kingdom.

...to the Lord, our God. We direct these prayers to God who is love, and who is present. God receives these prayers omni-directionally (in all directions and in no direction at the same time), being unconfined by time and space, thus connecting we the finite with He the infinite at a point of grace made manifest.

As we cleanse ourselves, and purify our minds and hearts for the riches that are to come within the Liturgy, the priest offers a general absolution as we have asked. He asks that this cleansing bring us to everlasting life, a life we can now enter unburdened, removed of that which binds. We give thanks for this mercy with the sign of the cross, so moved now to give glory to God in the highest, and peace to all on earth…

5

THE GLORIA

Having now been cleansed of sin, we are compelled to give thanks to God with this venerable hymn that dates back to the third century. Using the new text of the Roman Missal, in use since Advent 2011, let's shed light on this text and its place within the Introductory rites.

Glory to God in the highest, and on earth peace to people of good will...

When we begin the Gloria, we unite our voices to the song of the angels that announced the birth of Jesus. This announcing, given its present-day voicing, expresses more than a historical recalling, but rather the present reality of the birth of Jesus. It is a birth in a metaphorical sense, announcing the 'birth of Christ' gathered in the assembly of people, *in persona Christi* in the priest, and in the Word. The past nature of the original declamation transforms us into the present day choir of angels, announcing Christ's birth.

The Gloria continues:

...We praise you. We bless you. We adore you. We glorify you. We give you thanks for your great glory...

Five actions: praise, blessing, adoration, glorification, and giving thanks. Redundant? Perhaps the multiplicity of seemingly similar words symbolizes our inability to fully give thanks to God for the glory of all. Gratitude seems to be the overwhelming base sentiment, giving rise to the praise and blessing. Textually, we are grateful for the birth of Jesus, and for the subsequent Passion, through which we are redeemed. Perhaps our five senses cannot fully grasp the scope of or feel appropriate gratitude for the five wounds of Christ in his supreme act of redemption.

...Lord God, heavenly King, O God, Almighty Father. Lord Jesus Christ, Only Begotten Son, Lord God, Lamb of God, Son of the Father...

In this part of the Gloria, we see remnants of the penitential rite. Just as we sing "Lord, Christ, Lord have mercy," here we see the same parallel formula, beginning with the Father, the begotten Son, and the Lord God who is the Lamb of God. Naming both Father and Son as individuals in the first two lines, and then expressing the indivisibility of the Trinity in the third.

...You take away the sins of the world, have mercy on us; You take away the sins of the world, receive our prayer; You are seated at the right hand of the Father, have mercy on us...

Again, three references to mercy, or divine benevolence, as we sing of Christ's supreme mission, lived through his Passion. In the Gloria, we began with the birth of Jesus, gave inexpressible thanks for the indivisibility of the Father and Son, and now speak of his death and resurrection in the taking away of sin, and plead for mercy from the ascended Christ, now seated at the right hand of God.

...For you alone are the Holy One, you alone are the Lord, You

alone are the Most High, Jesus Christ, with the Holy Spirit, in the glory of God the Father. Amen.

We finish the Gloria with three uses of "you alone." 'Alone' signifying 'One,' giving glory and thanks to the Trinity and the infinite mystery of Three-in-One. We began at His birth and conclude with Pentecost, the whole of the Gospels. Glory and thanksgiving are woven throughout our gratitude for participating in this redemptive mystery we are called to enter. The nature of the mystery is then introduced in the next prayer of the priest, known as "the collect." "Let us pray…"

6

THE COLLECT

The collect (emphasis on the first syllable) is the prayer heard at Mass which always follows the Gloria and begins with the words: "Let us pray." The function of the collect is to unite (or collect) our individual prayers and bring to mind the character of a particular celebration. In the collect, this is voiced as a communal petition that directly relates to the given Holy Day, feast, or commemoration being celebrated.

(The USCCB has made a downloadable version of the current year's liturgical calendar available for free at: http://www.usccb.org/about/divine-worship/liturgical-calendar/.)

Beginning with "Let us pray," the collect follows with a brief period of silence. At this moment of silence — an intentional and formal component — we call to mind the petitions that we may have in our hearts at that time. The priest then makes a general petition on behalf of the gathered assembly which, we are called to remember, is a worldwide and universal assembly. In this petition, the priest asks that our lives become a reflection of Christ's, and that we become living embodiments of the Truth contained in the particular events being celebrated.

The collect concludes with a Trinitarian invocation, usually addressed to God the Father, through the Son, and in the Holy Spirit, again echoing the centrality of the Trinity in the foundation of our Faith.

Let's look at the collect for the feast of the Ascension as an example:

Let us pray... Silent prayer in which we mentally give voice to our petitions.

God our Father... A prayer directed to the Father.

...Make us joyful in the ascension of your Son Jesus Christ. May we follow him into the new creation, for his ascension is our glory and our hope... This communal petition aims at uniting our lives to that of Christ's life, so that we celebrate more than memory and historical events, but pray to make his glory our glory, and his hope our hope, right into the present moment, bridging the past with the present so that we can build the future in Him.

...We ask this through our Lord, Jesus Christ, your Son. Who lives and reigns with you and the Holy Spirit, One God forever and ever. Amen. We implore God, through Christ and the Holy Spirit to grant us these petitions which we have now 'collected'. The Trinitarian formula always makes mention of eternity, our hope and realization of a life lived in communion with Christ, prayed for in the above petition.

We have now completed our study of the Introductory

Rites of Mass. We began from the time we entered Church, and have progressed through a series of parts where we unified our minds, acknowledged our faults, sang of God's glory and mercy, and prayed for our lives to become united to Christ. We now have the proper mind and disposition to actively listen to the Word of God. Next, we will begin our study of the Liturgy of the Word.

7

SILENCE WITHIN THE LITURGY OF THE WORD

Having concluded our look at the Introductory rites, we move on to the Liturgy of the Word. Before we enter the first reading though, we pause for a moment of silence. To more fully understand why we are dedicating a chapter to talk about silence, consider this quote from the Church, found in *The General Instruction of the Roman Missal*:

> The Liturgy of the Word is to be celebrated in such a way as to promote meditation, and so any sort of haste that hinders recollection must clearly be avoided. During the Liturgy of the Word, it is also appropriate to include brief periods of silence, accommodated to the gathered assembly, in which, at the prompting of the Holy Spirit, the word of God may be

grasped by the heart and a response through prayer may be prepared. It may be appropriate to observe such periods of silence, for example, before the Liturgy of the Word itself begins, after the first and second reading, and lastly at the conclusion of the homily.

The Church is emphasizing the important communicative aspect of listening to the Word in Scripture and accomplishing this through a period of meditative silence. God speaks to us through words, yes, but also by the *"prompting[s] of the Holy spirit...grasped by [our] heart[s],"* or in other words, through the medium of silence. We petition, we praise, and then we are invited to stop and listen.

There's an art to listening, to being silent and allowing for stillness. And yet, to explain silence using words seems counterproductive, if not impossible. It's best when experienced. I'd like to share this brief mediation using Psalm 46:10 that I was introduced to a few years ago. It is a wonderful entrance into the beauty of silence.

After reading each line, take a slow breath in, and then slowly release.

Meditation on Psalm 46:10

Be still, and know that I am God. (breathe)
Be still, and know that I am. (breathe)
Be still and know. (breathe)
Be still. (breathe)
Be. (breathe)
silence.

8

THE FIRST READING

We have quieted our minds, and now we begin to listen to the Word of God. The Liturgy of the Word is comprised of an Old Testament reading, a psalm, and a Gospel reading. (The second reading, usually a letter of St. Paul's, we will look at separately.) The Old Testament reading and the Gospel harmonize with each other, and together reflect the theme being celebrated, in the context of the Liturgical season in which we find ourselves.

The first reading presents the first component of the fulfillment of God's plan, which is hope and promise. Keep in mind that the New Testament – the life of Christ – is the fulfillment of the prophets in the Old Testament. (That is why the Old Testament reading is sometimes referred to as the Prophecy.)

You often hear the term 'breaking bread'. Likewise, we can think of the readings as 'breaking open the Word'. Just as when breaking bread we gather around a table in community, so too when we break open the Word, we gather around the table of the Word. The ambo, from where the readings are read, can be thought of as the altar of the Word. This is in direct congruity with our Jewish brothers and sisters and their customs.

We might do well to consider how we listen. One can either listen passively or actively. If we listen actively, we hear, and we assimilate or take in what is being heard on several levels. We hear on a historical level of the events in the lives of the Israelites and their strife; but, more than in a mere history lesson, we assimilate the themes and struggles of the Israelites, and directly connect them to the here and now of our very own lives, as individuals, families, and communities. The face and reality of human struggles are fairly unchanged throughout the ages. If we listen passively, we have reduced the readings to a background sound, or to static. Our active or passive state creates our level of receptivity. How receptive are we to what is being read? How willing or able to relate?

And just a thought regarding the Liturgy of the Word as it relates to Christ telling us to have the mind of a child… Perhaps some of you were read to as children. Or perhaps you read to your children or grandchildren. That wonderful and intimate relationship of reader, listener, and story happens every Sunday. Maybe we were read a bedtime story or maybe we sat on someone's lap, wrapped in their arms, listening to a story. At Mass, we are wrapped in the warmth of God's arms, on the lap of God's church, reflected in the community with whom we celebrate. It's God's tender voice, reflected in the Word by the voice of the reader, and the story becomes Our Story. And just as the bedtime story gets us ready for bed, calming us, we are preparing for eternal life with God, through Christ, in being with the Holy Spirit.

9

THE PSALM

The book of Psalms is arguably the most human of the books in the Bible. The book of Psalms covers the entire continuum of human emotion and situations, ranging from praise to anger, joy to lament, and thanksgiving to pleading.

The psalms were used in worship in the Jewish temple, and so our own liturgical roots are clearly shown, and a Christological and messianic interpretation can be applied to them. Christ is the fulfillment of the psalms and prophets. Indeed, the psalm, within the context of the Liturgy, does just that: bridges the Old Testament with the New, as Christ became the fulfillment of the Old Testament prophets and psalmists.

Having just listened to the Old Testament reading, we follow with what has been called the *responsorial psalm*. There are a couple of salient points to remember about the nature of the psalm:

1.   The responsorial psalm is meant to **foster**

meditation upon the word of God. In this way, the psalm is bridge-forming, in a scriptural sense, between the Old Testament reading and the New Testament Gospel reading. It is our response to the Old Testament, and through our singing and listening, we meditate and prepare ourselves to hear the New Testament.

2. The 'response' nature of the responsorial psalm means that we not only respond to a cantor or a lector, but that we give a human **'response' to the scripture** that we have just heard, and how we view it in terms of our own salvation in Christ.

3. The emotive nature of the psalms may contradict how we personally feel. For example, how can we sing "O Lord, hear my cry" when we might happen to be in a perfectly fine and contented state? In this case, we would do well to remind ourselves of the **communal nature of the Mass**, and that we pray and meditate not only for ourselves, but for the greater community and faith family of which we are members through Baptism. Someone in our community is probably hurting and indeed crying out to God, and so for them, and through our realization that **we are that one body**, we should feel comfortable with the personal contradiction.

So far in the Liturgy of the Word, we have calmed our minds through silence, listened to the Old Testament reading, and internalized the promise and covenant of a people of antiquity. We have allowed ourselves to connect to these words, and meditated by walking the bridge of human response built upon the words of the psalmist. We will continue walking toward further nourishment and fulfillment in the Epistle, and finally the Gospel.

Next, we look at St. Paul and his epistles.

10

THE EPISTLE

The second reading, always from the New Testament, is often referred to as the epistle. An "epistle" is variously defined as being a letter, a missive, a communication, or a dispatch. The second reading, or epistle, that we hear at Mass is usually written by St. Paul, although this is not always the case. These epistles are letters that were written to early Christian groups and often contained Paul's teachings and advice to early Christians as they struggled with this radical new way of life. They varied in their degrees of formality, but always contained a teaching element and a sense of encouragement for continuing in the life of faith in Jesus Christ.

The fact that Paul wrote these letters is quite significant. Today, it is difficult to conceive of the weight these words must have carried, as modern technology is such that we can communicate with whomever we wish, no distance too great, with any number of communicative mediums. Generally speaking, we might admit to taking our communication very lightly at times. Rewind two thousand years and we can imagine how significant a letter, a formal means of communication, would have been to a group. What fervor and spirit Paul must have been filled with to write them! I would venture to guess that this Spirit was palpable in his words, felt by the recipients. The very voice that invited the rose to bloom must have invited him to write these letters. Could we say this about all of our communications and writings?

If we can assume that the Holy Spirit was involved in the penning of these letters, we can reason that since the Holy Spirit (sent by Christ) exists beyond the confines of time and space, then these messages and words must also carry with them a timeless relevance. These letters, despite being written for a particular group in a particular historical time, carry just as much relevance for our lives today. For when is love not the greatest of these, or when are we not one body, or when does hope not disappoint (to quote a few Paul-isms)? These are timeless dictums, always applicable to our lives as Christians, during our struggles in leading the Christian life, and heard at the place where time and timeless meet: in the Liturgy.

From the struggles, promises, and hopes of a wandering people of the Old Testament, to our own human response to the Psalms, we receive inspired encouragement from a letter, surely written to us. In listening to the reading of this epistle, we prepare ourselves to hear the teachings of our teacher through the words and example of his life and sacrifice. How can we respond with anything else but Alleluia?

11

ALLELUIA

Before we hear the Gospel and drink the life-giving words and works of Christ, we – in an act of reverence – stand and sing the Alleluia. The Alleluia is a response that has sprung forth from our hearing of the Old Testament, our resonance with the Psalm, and the sharing of our Christian lives in the New Testament Reading. A bit of history first…

Our present day 'Alleluia' comes from the Hebrew word '*Halleluyah*', literally meaning to "praise (joyously, even rapturously), Yahweh." Alleluia, both as an expression of praise and thanksgiving, has been incorporated into our liturgies, particularly apropos in the Easter Season, because of its praise and joyous nature, and historically because of the 'Alleluia psalms' that were chanted during the Passover time in the Jewish tradition. Evidence of our Jewish heritage colors much of our Liturgy, as we will continue to see. Also interesting to note, the term '*Halleluyah*' has similar etymological roots as the Arabic '*Alhamdulillah*' used in the Islamic tradition. So 'praise to God' has a far reaching history, and one can see in our common roots the ecumenical potential.

As a matter of form, the Alleluia as a part of the Liturgy has a meditative quality, as it was the liturgical office of a cantor and choir to sing, accompanying a procession of the book of Gospels. The meditative nature of the Alleluia was to prepare the mind and heart for the reading of the Gospel. The long and flowing quality of the music, namely in the Gregorian form, had the wafting (almost musical-incense) aesthetic and easily led one into the proper frame of mind to drink forth from the Gospel.

Since the Second Vatican Council, we have seen a popular trend to make the Alleluia more into a congregational acclamation of triple alleluias, deriving from the Easter Vigil pre-Vatican II rite when the priest would intone, or begin by singing, a triple alleluia before the Gospel. This was never a mandate as much as it was a liturgical trend which is now almost ubiquitous.

A brief Gospel verse often echoes the theme that appears in the Gospel, and is often a direct quote from the Gospel to be read. This was also performed by a cantor, and still retains that tradition. The Alleluia praise is sung once more after this verse, and proper praise has been given for the Gospel we are about to hear.

It's worth noting that we give thanks and praise before we hear the Gospel. This is reflective of the hope, *which does not disappoint* (thank you, St. Paul!), that Christ *will* fulfill the promise of the Old Testament, and will be our shelter and stronghold for which we cried out in the Psalms. We give thanks because we *know*, and our standing and singing of the Alleluia is a statement of that faith.

12

THE GOSPEL

We have now reached the pinnacle of the Liturgy of the Word, namely, the Gospel: the teachings and the life of Jesus. The word *gospel* itself literally means "good news," and was taken from the Greek word '*euangelion*', meaning "good message." You can also see the connection in the modern English word "evangelist": those who bear the good message.

The Gospel is held in such esteem that we stand for its reading, a sign of reverence for our encounter with Christ, believed to be present in the Word. The deacon, properly ordained as the proclaimer of the Word, receives a blessing from the priest, asking worthiness to proclaim this news of inestimable goodness. The *Book of Gospels*, separate from the Lectionary containing the first two readings, is held high (significantly, it is elevated at the same place as the bread and wine later in the Mass) so that all might behold. As we sing 'Alleluia', the book is processed to the ambo, the place designated for the readings. The ambo can be thought of as an 'altar of the Word'. (Remember that we processed the book into the church at the very beginning of Mass, so this is not the first encounter we have had with the *Book of Gospels.*)

Further esteem for the Gospel is frequently expressed, especially for high solemnities, when the Gospel is incensed, a symbol of our prayers rising up to the Lord. Often two candle bearers will stand to either side of the ambo, a sign of reverence to be sure, but also symbolic of the light of Christ, dispeller of darkness, so present in the Word(s) we hear.

The messages contained in the life and teachings of Jesus Christ are so powerful that after the deacon announces the Gospel, we trace the sign of the cross on our heads, lips, and heart as we say "Glory to you, Lord." As we give God this glory, we are asking for these words to be in our minds and present in our thoughts. We implore the words we hear to be the words we speak as we trace our lips. Finally, we trace the cross on our hearts so the word of God can be present in our hearts. The love of Christ present in the Gospel can be the same love that we carry in our own hearts, such that it begets our thoughts and words.

After these introductory words and deeds, the Word (gospel) is proclaimed, which is to say, the gospel passage is read aloud. Afterwards, when the deacon announces that what we have heard is "The Gospel of the Lord," again, we offer our praise by responding with, "Praise to you, Lord Jesus Christ." At this point the deacon kisses the Word, offering yet another parallel between the Altar, reverenced with a kiss at the beginning, the Eucharist, and the nourishment of the Word.

The four evangelists – Matthew, Mark, Luke and John – offer us different perspectives, and highlight different aspects of Christ, his life, and his teachings. The liturgical year, divided into cycles A, B, and C after the Second Vatican Council, gives us ample opportunity to hear more of the riches of the gospels. In cycle A years, we hear from Matthew, who focuses greatly on Christ's ministry in terms of his fulfillment of the prophecies. In cycle B years, the humanity of Christ is emphasized with readings from Mark. Luke's passages, which we read in cycle C years, are an encounter with a merciful and healing savior. Readings from the Gospel of John are used for solemnities and high liturgical seasons such as Easter, and his particular gospel emphasizes deeper theological truths – for example, the Eucharistic discourse of chapter 6. These gospels, timeless as they are, had specific target audiences in mind even when they were written.

Though we process in with the Gospels, we do not process the Book out of the Church, leaving it instead at the ambo. Symbolically, we carry the Word, now present in our mind, lips, and hearts, into the world, in turn becoming bearers of the gospels – evangelists. So in this sense then, yes, we do process the *Book of Gospels* out of Mass, charged with the task of furthering the Kingdom (and safely navigating the parking lot).

13

THE HOMILY

I have heard it said that the average attention span lasts for six seconds. I am sure this refers to complete, razor-like focus by a listener. Regardless, this has to be a daunting statistic for a homilist, charged with the task of combining the ingredients of the scriptures of a given Mass into a concrete and cohesive recipe for assimilating the words of the Scriptures and guiding us on how to implement them into our own lives in such a way that it nourishes us and the world around us.

The idea of the homily is fairly brilliant. We have (actively) listened to the Old Testament, a Psalm, an Epistle, sang Alleluia, and heard a Gospel passage. Five different scripture passages meant to inform and influence our lives so as to reflect Christ's life, can be quite a bit to take in during the brief span of their reading. The brain, holding all these readings in our short term memory, doesn't have the time necessary to bring this information to the frontal cortex of the brain, where it becomes long term memory, capable of transformative learning, dictating our very being, thought, word, and deed. So we rely on and trust a priest or deacon, whose vocations ask for assimilation of these readings, to enlighten us and interpret these scriptures into real life applicability, trusting that their prayer over the readings has lead to a message we can take into our Monday through our Saturday.

And let's face it, we never lose that childlike sense of, "but why?" or "how come?". The urge that compels us to question why our 7-year-old self has to come in at dark is the same urge that compels us now to ask, "What do these readings have to do with my life today?" Instead of barreling through these readings during the Mass, it just makes sense to stop and simply ask that question. "How does this apply to my life?" This is the raison d'être of the homily.

Priest and deacons take *homiletics*, classes on how to make an effective homily (in an allotted eight minutes). They pore over the readings to find a salient point, and to make modern-day sense out of the timeless truth expressed in these scriptures. The dynamic between homilist and listener is a delicate one: Has the homilist's reflection merited your attention? What is the dynamic between the 'interesting-factor' of the homily and our ability to actively listen? What makes for a memorable homily? Honestly, how well have we listened? Do we understand the difference between active and passive listening?

Having known many priests and deacons, I can tell you that the homily is viewed as a sacred task, and one not taken lightly. Even priests who have been homilizing for many years still pray and seek freshness from these accounts in the Scripture, and they care intensely and deeply that they can extract a message that you can take into your lives. And having known many deacons, I cannot fully express the passion that deacons share in their role of sharing their reflections on these sacred words.

So in the homily we pause after having heard Truth. We stop to grasp the reality which has been faithfully and prayerfully discerned by the homilist. Priests and deacons spend hours a week praying over these words. We can give eight minutes, right?

14

THE CREED

I thought hard about the best way to present information about the Creed in this chapter, and instead of going line by line and dealing with each morsel of truth individually, I will try to paint a larger picture about what is happening during this part of the Mass. Why is the Creed directly after the Readings? Why is it before the Eucharist and prayers of the faithful? Why is *'catholic'* spelled with a lower case 'c'? Why do we bow at "and by the power of the Holy Spirit"?

Belief, represented in a creed, is something we hold to be true. Something we hold to be true stands as a constant. It is a point of reference in a world of confusion, untruth, and illusion. Our belief in one God allows us to see the unreality of those things in our lives that we treat like many, mini-gods. I use the first line in the Creed just as an example. Other lines in the Creed equally dispel the illusion that those things in our world that we set up as gods and to which we become slaves hold any significance or truth.

Consider, too, that we recite the Creed together, in unison. The unity of our prayer, when we recite the Creed, confirms this truth: The unity of a multitude of voices is greater than the summation of individual voices.

Just prior to the recitation of the Creed, we listen as the readings, psalm, and Gospel passage create the words that become the foundation of our belief. This belief forms our faith, and our faith forms our lives. In the unity of our faith, lived out in our lives, we become embodiments of truth, and this truth is a realization of our communion with God, with the saints, and with the forgiveness of sins. We become one and catholic – truly universal. Individual distinction disappears into universal (i.e., catholic with a small 'c') oneness, and love permeates the seen and unseen, as was exemplified and spoken of by Christ, who indeed showed one in being-ness with the Father.

"By the power of the Holy Spirit, He came down from Heaven." We bow, in the same motion of Christ's descent, a descent "for us and for our salvation," but also reverencing the gift given to us in Christ's human suffering. He was destined to suffer and die, the paradoxical gift of death for life. The intimate relationship between death and life is almost such that there is no difference. Is not dying to self true life? And isn't eternal life given to us through death? Strange indeed, but Christ's gift of self gives us the example *par excellence* of service, of dying, and of love. He sets the standard for the unconditional. Our lives then should be, if nothing else, a bow of gratitude for His example of selflessness: He bowed His head to die, in the name of oneness and love.

This one, holy, catholic, and apostolic vision engenders a joy of resurrection, promised in our belief, foretold in the Gospel, and lived in the present in our own lives. If lived in

His, our everlasting life is assured. The world, without end, will become a kingdom – a kingdom within, outside, and without end, forever and ever. This profession, which precedes the Eucharist, illuminates these words with a light that dispels the darkness of doubt and endows us with a task of the angels: Be messengers of truth.

15

THE PRAYERS OF INTERCESSION (PETITIONS)

There's something so strikingly beautiful about the petitions, properly called "the prayer of the faithful." Perhaps it is the oneness that they signify, or the humbling of a community, who by their very voicing of petitions, acknowledge a need and reliance upon God. To hear hundreds of voices as one saying, "Lord, hear our prayer," one hears the voices of deep faith realizing the words in the scripture passage "ask and you shall receive."

As a rule, there are four intentions that are required to be in the petitions:

1. The needs of the worldwide church;
2. Public authorities and worldwide salvation;
3. For those burdened with physical, mental, or situational difficulty; and

4.   For the local community.

We ask guidance for those in Church leadership positions, namely: the pope, cardinals, and all who teach the faith. Tied intimately to church, we pray for the Spirit to illuminate the minds of state officials throughout the world, down to our own communities. As much as the idea of a separation of Church and state may seem appealing in a democracy, we have to acknowledge at some level gray areas of inevitable crossings, and so we pray for, instead of bemoan, civic leadership. And just as Jesus cared for the sick and marginalized, so too do we pray for those in the community facing needs. Other petitions may certainly be added. After all, these are the prayers of the faithful...our prayers and our needs.

It might be worth considering that these are prayers of the *faithful*, those who are full of faith. The voicing of the prayer marks only the beginning of the prayer's life. After we have given voice to the prayers, we do our part by having faith, in fact, being *full of faith* that these prayers, or intercessions, have been heard. Being full of faith directly counters being full of doubt, which disables our ability to 'hear' God's answers.

Have you ever stopped to think just where these prayers go? Do we imagine them to go 'up'? Just where are the 'ears' of God? Are they heard 'up there' or are they manifested 'within'? Do they have any specific course or direction? Our finite nature crying out to a God that is beyond place, beyond here and now, and beyond all time appears to limit our ability to communicate, yet the Liturgy speaks clearly to this, acknowledging the presence of God within the community, in the Word, and in the Eucharist. It's where the timeless meets that which is within time, and prayers' answers are revealed within all senses and outside of senses.

So perhaps our concluding prayer for the petitions should become, 'Lord, teach us to listen,' so that we hear, not in an exclusively auditory way, but in such a way that our 'hearing' becomes a synonym for knowing. This knowing, an experience of the Divine, of God's presence within each of us, empowers. And if God's presence is within all, I believe when we speak "Lord, hear our prayer," we are entreating God *through* the ears (both literally and metaphorically) of the people with whom we gather, whereby we are both commissioners and commissioned, through promptings of the spirit in a worshiper – 'faith-filled' to become the very instruments that God uses to answer. Through grace we can have prayers answered *through* us, as we live our Christian lives and further the kingdom. God uses us to become embodiments of the answers to the prayers heard.

So for the needs of the church, state, those in need of help, and for all we encounter, for all those prayers we hold in our hearts, and for the prayers that we have never given word or voice to, we pray to the Lord, and ask the Lord to hear our prayers. Then, we listen, not with ears alone, but with our beings. Being full of faith, we allow God to answer through us and through others, living the reality of One, in the Body of Christ we now prepare to receive and become.

This concludes the Liturgy of the Word portion of Mass.

16

THE OFFERTORY

As we continue our look at the individual parts of the Mass, we build a bridge between the Liturgy of the Word and the Liturgy of the Eucharist with the preparation of the gifts (the offertory). This offertory is one of three processions during the mass. (The other two are the entrance and communion processions.) The offertory chant or song may accompany this procession.

Much happens at this point in our Liturgy. Gifts, which come from the community and are offered before God, are collected and brought before the altar by ministers. We offer to God that which has been given to us. At the same time, the altar is prepared with the placing of the corporal (a 'smaller' altar cloth used out of a mindfulness and reverence of Eucharistic particles), the purificators, the Missal (containing the prayers for the Eucharist) and the chalice(s).

The priest and servers meet those who represent the

community and receive the gifts that will become the Body and Blood of Christ. The communal origin of the gifts of bread and wine – the "work of human hands" – is significant. The bread, which becomes the bread of life, and the wine, which becomes our "spiritual drink" allowing us to "share in the divinity of Christ," have profound and very real ramifications. What does it mean to share in Christ's divinity, as is prayed at every Mass?

By offering these gifts, we ask to share in Christ's divinity and transform the bread and wine into Body and Blood so that we can eat and drink true divine LIFE and divine TRUTH. Christ demanded of us that we "take and eat...take and drink." If he wanted us to have the option, he might have added "...that is, if you feel like it." He wanted us to take and eat so that we could *become*, (You are what you eat?) so that his work on earth – spreading the kingdom – could continue. This is no small charge. So when we offer the bread and wine to become our spiritual food and drink, we offer ourselves at the same time so that we can continue to be the Body of Christ, transforming ourselves and the world.

Together we pray that these gifts may be acceptable and that they not only transform us, but the entire church, and ultimately the world. And while not taking anything away from the presence in the Eucharist, keep in mind that, though not present on the altar, this prayer is also for our monetary gifts, our gifts of stewardship, and indeed all gifts that we offer, that they may be "for the praise and glory of his name, for our good and for the good of all the Church." In a small way, just as Christ offered himself as ransom for the world, we offer ourselves – mind, body and spirit – to continue being the light of Christ to a world experiencing darkness.

The priest then offers a prayer over the gifts. This prayer

changes each day, depending upon the nature of the feast or celebration. At this point, we begin the Eucharistic Prayer. This prayer is made up of eight sections, each of which we will look at in turn.

17

THE EUCHARISTIC PRAYER

The portion of the Mass that begins after the Offertory and goes through the final doxology and Amen is known properly as the Eucharistic Prayer. It can be conceived of as having eight parts. The first part is expressed as a prayer of thanksgiving. This offering of thanks during the Eucharistic Prayer begins with the (now) familiar dialogue:

The Lord be with you. And with your spirit.
Lift up your hearts. We lift them up to the Lord.
Let us give thanks to the Lord our God. It is right and just.

The above dialogue, which reaffirms the rightness and goodness of giving thanks and praise, is known as the preface of the Eucharistic Prayer. It is appropriate to the season or feast which is being celebrated (i.e., it changes from one liturgical season, feast, etc. to the next) and segues into the 'song of the angels', the Sanctus. But first, a word about thanksgiving and gratitude…

I have heard it said that to live in a state of gratitude is to live in a state a prayer. Gratitude is such that once you allow yourself to be grateful for one thing, you end up becoming grateful for everything *ad infinitum*. Take your morning cup of coffee. If you're grateful for that, then you must also be grateful for the money you had to purchase it, for the job that gave you that opportunity, for the seller, for the distributor, for the crafter of the mug, for the picker of the coffee, for the grower, for the earth which provided the coffee bean and the water, for the Creator, and so on. Indeed everything leads to Everything. You begin to see the interconnectivity and beautiful design of the world and of life. Gratitude becomes all consuming if not overwhelming. Every simple expression of gratitude is then also an unspoken expression of gratitude for all of life.

Back in the Liturgy, it is this endless thanks that we offer. It is noteworthy that we give thanks *after* we offer (i.e., after the Offertory). The action of offering our gifts and ourselves is followed directly by, and intricately connected to, giving thanks. We are thankful for the opportunity to offer. This thanksgiving becomes thanks for Christ and for His supreme offering, as well as its relation to the goodness of the earth and God's creation. This thanksgiving flows out and becomes cosmic and timeless, as we join with the saints and the angels in *their*, now *our*, song of praise. This becomes yet another instant of past dissipating into the present so that there is only one moving, infinite moment of endless thanks to God, with praise organically emanating from our thanks.

This thread of thanksgiving in the Eucharistic Prayer – indeed what *Eucharist* literally means – is continually woven throughout the remainder of this prayer and the Liturgy, leading into thanks for Christ's sacrifice. This is so that later our reception of Holy Communion, received in thanksgiving, stirs within us the desire to "share in Christ's divinity," such that our acts of kindness and love become a physical manifestation of Eucharist. Eucharist then becomes a verb, a way of being. And the way of living in a state of Eucharist is indeed to be living in a state of prayer.

18

SANCTUS (HOLY)

So we just gave complete and total thanks in the first part of the Eucharistic Prayer, and now we sing with the angels…

Holy, holy, holy Lord God of host.
Heaven and earth are full of your glory. (Isaiah 6:3)
Hosanna in the highest.
Blessed is He who comes in the name of the Lord,
Hosanna in the highest.(Matthew 21:9)

The word hosanna comes etymologically from the Hebrew word '*Hoshana*', meaning to appeal for salvation or help. It's a cry for help that has come to mean adoration or praise. It's interesting that the same word can have two seemingly opposite meanings: one being a cry for help, the other being an exuberant acclamation of praise. Does this indicate a similarity between a cry and acclamation, or does it merely indicate the coexistent nature of these seemingly polemic emotional states? Either way — cry or praise, or everything between — one thing is certain, and that is complete and total acknowledgement and surrender to God.

But what about the word 'Holy'? I always found it strange to call God holy, not because it wasn't true, but because it seemed so obvious that He was: Holy, sacred (Sanctus), worthy of devotion. I reasoned, as a child, that maybe it was a good thing to say something obvious. Otherwise why would we tell those we love that we love them? They know it, right? I think we do it because it is almost like an involuntary action. In the same way that you blink if your finger comes toward your eye, you express love when you are overwhelmed by it. And by the time we come to the Sanctus, if we haven't become overwhelmed with love for God, having just previously expressed our unending and inexpressible thanks, than perhaps part of us just remained closed. Our love and our crying 'holy' is the 'blink' when God's love approaches our 'eye' (heart?). Digging deeper…

Heaven and earth can be thought of as opposites, as a poetic tool used to indicate the infinite, the circular distance between two opposites so that their individuality dissipates into oneness (kingdom of God). Heaven and earth…what else is there? It's saying that everything is glory. God's glory is an extension of Himself, implying God is all and in all, in the expansion and the infinite in-between of heaven and earth.

And highest? Praise and acclamation to the highest, to heaven, to our thought of the 'where' of God. *In* the highest… the angels, saints and all who have come before also express praise from heaven, our upward local thought of God. Our voice becomes their voice and it becomes *one* voice. Just as heaven and earth become all expressively, so do *our* and *their* become one. And finally, think of the phrase "take the high road." This means take the road of 'higher consciousness', the right thing, possibly the 'Christ-like' action. Using either interpretation, hosanna in the highest is praise stemming from thought and meditation upon the wonder of God so that when we are at this level all we can do is shout for praise and acclamation for everything, including our cries for help, and the infinite in-between.

So overwhelmed with God's word and with thanksgiving, we can't help but express just how holy, sacred, and worthy of praise God is. Praise! Absolute praise in the highest level of thought – meditation upon God's wonder. And "blessed is he who comes in the name of the Lord." Our lives and our actions become an act of thanksgiving, coming in the name of the Lord. Every kind deed we do becomes a waving of a palm branch and a shout of Hosanna! Hosanna!

Blessed is He, and blessed are you, who lives in the name of the Lord.

19 & 20

EPICLESIS & INSTITUTION

After we have joined with the angels and saints in their endless song of praise, the priest, on behalf of all gathered, invokes the Holy Spirit to "come down upon these gifts." The word *'epiclesis'* literally translates into 'invocation', or a calling down upon. Followed closely to this is the institution narrative, where we remember and recall "the night before he died." Each of the elements, bread and wine, are offered. We take, and we eat, in memory of him.

I include both of these in the same chapter primarily because the order of these two elements, *epiclesis* and the institution narrative, are reversed in the Eastern rites. In the Roman rite, the consecration (transubstantiation) is believed to take place during the institution narrative. In the East, it is believed to take place with the *epiclesis*, coming after the institution, with the invoking of the Holy Spirit. Though there is obviously debate surrounding the form and order, perhaps we might be so bold as to proffer that it does not actually matter when, or even how, this change occurs. Rather, let us rejoice that it *does* become the Body and Blood of Christ. As they say, substance over form…

So in our Roman Rite, the priest asks the blessing of the Holy Spirit by way of outstretched arms and the signing of the cross, to sanctify the gifts; to make them holy. We then recall the night he was betrayed and are shown the depth of his love in the prayer of institution.

He gave You thanks and praise… (always start with gratitude).

The body given up for you… (insert your name here)

The blood shed for you and for all… (insert your name here, too)

Do this in memory of me… (how will **you** live this memory?)

A dear deacon friend of mine shared some words he whispers to himself during the consecration. When the bread is elevated, he says, "By your broken body, I am made whole." When the cup is elevated, he says, "By your blood shed, I am washed clean." It seems like such a paradox. A broken body making us whole, and blood washing us clean. But paradoxes speak such deep truths.

(We exist in a world of so many seeming contradictions, and we use the juxtaposition of opposites to grasp reality. When we are at our most broken, from where does our wholeness come? When we are covered in the filth of our own egos, how are we washed clean? To this end, when others are less than whole, what is our role in restoring wholeness?)

So now the bread and wine have become the Body and Blood.

Stop what you're doing right now and think about this. Theologians, mystics, saints, and sinners have written extensively on the Presence of the Eucharist and what it means to them. What would you write?

May our memory of Him be His reality in Us.

21

THE ANAMNESIS

The mystery of faith…

The *anamnesis* is our 'remembering', or calling to mind. Frequently in life, when things happen that seem miraculous, they are often accompanied by a flood of memories that appear to fall in perfect order. They offer an ideal path by which the only possible outcome could be what now is. This is what happens when the bread and wine become Body and Blood. We proclaim the mystery of faith, and the memory (or remembering) is the totality of Christ's ministry: dying, rising, and coming again. The miracle before us could not have come by any other way. It ties the past to the future (coming again) through the present medium of the Body and Blood. The new translation of the Mass, which began Advent 2011, offers three choices for this, and each has a different color of the *mysterium fidei*, the mystery of faith.

"We proclaim your death, O Lord, and profess your Resurrection

until you come again."

This acclamation denotes an activity upon our part: that of proclaiming and professing the death and resurrection. It gives a time period: until you come again. Proclaiming and professing does not stop at the material vocalization, but points to a way of life that we bring to our lives. We promise to profess the dying and rising, and everything in between, in our very own lives. How will you proclaim His death?

"When we eat this Bread and drink this Cup, we proclaim your death, O Lord, until you come again."

This acclamation is centered upon the sacramental reality of the Eucharist. By our belief and reception of communion, we profess and proclaim Christ as a transformative power and an agent of change within this world – specifically in the power of the Presence in the Eucharist. The Eucharist, being the source and summit of our faith, gives us spiritual strength to proclaim unendingly.

"Save us, Savior of the world, for by your Cross and Resurrection, you have set us free."

This acclamation is curious. It's both a statement and a plea. It's a plea for salvation from the known Savior. It both reaches into the past and pleads for something that's been done already (salvation). We recognize that by the Cross and Resurrection, the world has been saved, but what of the present statement 'save us'? Why would be asked to be saved when later we proclaim ourselves to be saved? Perhaps the acclamation implies our active role in our salvation, and the continual need to ask for Christ's guidance in our lives. Certainly we all find ourselves with our white flags in the air from time to time. Being saved is not necessarily a one time event. Salvation is a gift that requires continual upkeep and maintenance. (To borrow from the lexicon of theater, every once in a while we need to say, "Line please.")

Perhaps you are asking why "Christ has died, Christ is risen, Christ will come again" is no longer included in the anamnesis. In the new translation, this was left out for the reason of tense. The whole Eucharistic Prayer is addressed to God in second person. This acclamation grammatically broke tense to speak of Christ in the third person. This update to form is a matter of consistency and a faithfulness to earlier translations.

Let us proclaim the mystery.

22

THE OFFERING

The offering within the Eucharistic Prayer acknowledges our calling to mind the mystery of our faith and then puts forth the reason for the mystery, the reason for the entire sacrifice of the spotless victim and lamb: unity within the Spirit.

The Eucharistic prayers, of which there are four, ask that this sacrifice be accepted for the purpose of absolute unity. This notion of unity, through the grace of the Holy Spirit, cannot be de-emphasized. Christ's arms on the cross embraced the world in its entirety; with no exception. (Does rain discriminate who it falls upon?)

However, unity cannot be thought of as just a physical proximity of peoples who happen to stand beneath the banner of a specific creed or doctrine, within the same building or conceptual framework at some given time. If this was the case, we may as well just all gather together in one physical place and give one big group hug. Jesus put forth a much more profound vision of unity when he called for us to be one.

This commission of unity, through the sacrifice of His own body and blood, is a unity not of bodily proximity but of spiritual like-mindedness founded in the virtues he embodied. A sacrifice, by its very nature, is offered for someone or something. We are that for which the sacrifice has been offered. Sacrifices traditionally have been offered to gods or overly demanding deities. This is an absolute reversal. Christ is sacrificed to *us*! Our insistence on living with a worshipping attitude toward our separateness and division was our own godly and selfish demand for this sacrifice. Well, God gave it to us, and the arms that were outstretched on the cross embrace us still, though we demanded the sacrifice.

We pray for God to accept this offering of bread and wine, but will we accept what Christ has offered to us? If so, how? It is said that love is the impulse toward unity. If we truly believe the words of Saint Paul that we are one unified body, no one excluded, how on earth can we justify exclusion of any kind? If unity is perfect love realized, how can we ever dare rest? Talk is quite cheap. How will we express our gratitude for this embrace?

Until we can act and react with absolute love and compassion, unconditionally towards all of our brothers and sisters, Catholic and non-Catholic, Christian and non-Christian, how can we possibly say that we have completed the biblical dictum that "all may be as one"? It does not seem possible, or even desirable, to have partial unity. Partial unity is not unity at all. Perhaps a glimpse of unity, but certainly not full unity. Unity is unity.

At this point in the Liturgy, in the Eucharistic Prayer, the bread and wine have become the Body and Blood. It has become Christ offered to us. He died so that we might live. And we live so that we might give death to that which divides: discrimination, judgmental views, assumptions, sexism, racism, and the list goes on. If we truly believe and subscribe to what Christ taught, then our walking up the aisle to receive communion is a sign of commitment to that cause and a promise to work toward unity. It seems simple, but how often do we realize that to work for unity means to work *against* division? How often do we smugly rest on the veneer of our individualities as people and communities? How often do we love to categorize ourselves and others into convenient conceptual compartments?

We offer much more than bread and wine. We offer ourselves and say, yes, I will continue your work, Christ. You gave everything so that I might live. You accepted the stranger and the outcast, fed the hungry, clothed the naked, gave food to the poor, all to show that we are all one. I am going to receive you in the Eucharist, and when I leave this morning (afternoon, evening...), I promise to pick up where you left off. You have my word.

So that all may be one.

23

THE INTERCESSION

Picking up from the previous chapter where we offered *ourselves*, as we offered the Body and Blood for unity through Christ and the grace of the Spirit, we come to the intercessory portion of the Eucharistic prayers. Mindful that there is a different wording for each of the four prayers, the general ethos remains the same, and the essential truth of our faith permeates each of them.

One general theme of this intercession, and the entire Sacrifice of the Mass, is made clear in its insistence on communion with everyone. It is here that we are asked to pray for the Pope, bishops, clergy, and all the people throughout the world. We pray in communion with all who have gone before us, some marked with the sign of faith, and those *"whose faith is known to You alone."* We acknowledge union with the saints, the angels, and the Virgin Mary. We acknowledge those who seek, those who are here, and all children everywhere. Have we left anyone out? I believe the point of the intercession is fairly clear: When Christ came to offer himself to all, he came to offer himself to the totality of humanity.

A second theme provides us with our *raison d'être* for this prayer: a vision of glory, to sing with every creature in the kingdom, light, happiness, and peace in God's presence. Later, we will say so even more specifically when, together, we pray that "thy kingdom come." We ardently desire to be in the kingdom. We ask not just for ourselves. We ask for everyone, without division, to share in this light. What Christ offers to us – a way paved with truth and life – by his death, was paved for all because he 'loved the world so much'. As far as I know, no exceptions or asterisks were inserted here. And when we can live so that there is no Gentile or Jew, woman or man, and all such dualistic division is eliminated, perhaps this is when our lives become a true song of glory.

Are we willing to live toward this? To live this way is to encounter the kingdom. It's to see a vision of glory and be completely blinded by the light of peace and happiness. We should be stumbling over each other to receive this communion, our hearts so enraptured with desire to be blinded.

Soon we will receive. We will *"grow in Love."* This will cause us to *"advance in peace."* With each peaceful advancement, the light shines that much brighter. Light passes on. The darkness of separation dissipates. When light is given, the giver does not lose any of his/her light. The receiver becomes the giver becomes the receiver *ad infinitum* until there is only light, and we have all received the light of Christ.

Our reception of communion confirms our commitment to let Christ transform our lives into a living light.

May we be blinded so that we can finally see as one.

24

THE FINAL DOXOLOGY & AMEN

The final doxology, an acclamation of praise, has a Trinitarian dimension in its mention of the Father, Son, and the Holy Spirit. Let's explore the words, their relationship to what happens before and after, and the wordless truth towards which the words lead us.

In the last chapter we found the *who* of the Eucharistic Prayer, and found a litany of angels, saints, faithfully departed, and those whose faith is known only to God, all within the embrace of a crucified Christ. We have to assume that God would then want all — the entire communion of spirits, from all space, time, and history — to enter into this doxology, for reasons I hope will become evident.

'*Through*' him has significance when we think of the meaning of the word '*through*'. From the Latin '*per*' it can mean '*by means of*', or causing instrumentality to something or someone, namely, Him. So we could think of '*through him*' as meaning '*because of him*'. Christ is the instrument, and a song of salvation is sung by his life. But it also has a destination aspect. '*Through*' denotes a beginning point, a way. But there is not necessarily an ending point as much as a point that is reached and then continued. In this sense, what might it mean if we move *through* him? Christ becomes a place in which me move through, going to a place where we continue, but still *with* him.

'*With*' him then takes on a decidedly relational aspect. The way that we have gone through continues now *with* him. The *way*, now becomes the *life*, characterized by him with whom we now proceed. Now that we have gone through, and continue, *truth* now becomes present as we find our selves *in* him.

'*In*' him invokes a profound degree of intimacy to the point of unity or at oneness with. It has an aspect of totality in such a way that when we are *in* him, we cannot be anywhere else at the same time. This is the *truth* of communion with Christ. When we receive, we become. And what we become, by allowing ourselves this transformation, is an embodiment of *Truth*. When this happens, our *truth* then influences our *lives* so that we can lead others to the *way* through Him. Thus, we can achieve unity. This unity is certainly the hope of our entire Eucharistic Prayer, and indeed our Eucharistic existence.

So just as the spirit descended upon the apostles, the spirit now descends upon us, threading all together, through our unifying acts of charity and love, which happen naturally. These unifying acts are an outgrowth of our having gone *through*, *with*, and *in*. Christ gives us an unfailing method to bring us to unity with the Spirit. We need only allow it to happen by removing our 'self' from the scene. And when we do, and we behold the scene now present in our selfless unity, how can we do anything else by give all glory and honor to God?

So we give glory and honor, finding ourselves singing an endless song of praise, a promised aspect of the kingdom of God, in a kingdom of timelessness and love without conditions. When there are no conditions to love, time disappears, and we come face to face with the everlasting. Lasting, of course, forever and ever. Amen.

25

THE LORD'S PRAYER (OUR FATHER)

"In the words our savior gave us..."
                                    Our Father...

The word 'our' immediately takes this prayer from a personal statement to a communal prayer. We pray to *our* Father. Just as one does not choose his father or mother, so, too, one does not choose a spiritual Father from where we "move and have our being." While one can certainly deny a relation, no denial can erase one's sonship or daughterhood. Our identity as children of God remains therefore unalterable. Carried to its conclusion, *'brothers and sisters in Christ'* becomes much more than a poetic metaphor. It becomes a reality of complete and unbreakable familial unity.

                           ...Who art in heaven...

If God is in heaven, and at the same time within us, how does that affect our notion of heaven? What is your perception of heaven?

...Hallowed be thy name...

The name of God, so revered as to remain unspoken in many traditions, and specifically not to be taken in vain, holds within it a vibratory power. To speak the name of God, and meditate upon the name of God, is to wrap oneself in belief. Names, by their nature, represent something or someone. What truth does the name of God signify?

...Thy Kingdom come...

If one thinks of a kingdom, perhaps a 'place' separate from ourselves comes to mind. But how can a place move from where it is, in an active state of 'coming'? So must it be our 'going' to the kingdom rather than the kingdom coming to us? But, Christ specified that the kingdom was doing the moving. What if the kingdom was not so much a place external to us, but rather a 'place' inside of us, revealed when we follow Christ? Might the kingdom come to us when we remove what might prevent its revelation?

...Thy will be done on earth as it is in heaven...

The will of God, discernible within us, if prayerfully followed, will 'bring' the kingdom so that our lives will become a series of interconnected kingdom moments. These moments are as seamless as our ability to discern, listen, and allow a spirit of unity within the spirit to become us. Might this not be heavenly?

...Give us this day our daily bread...

This is an entreaty for all things necessary to sustain us in the **present** moment: food, shelter, clothing, community. Again, a prayer to give us daily bread implies that if we have more than our daily bread, we 'feed' those who do not. How much do we really need?

...And forgive us our trespasses as we forgive those who trespass against us...

An entreaty for cleansing from **past** transgressions, but the condition we place upon ourselves here – "as we forgive" – cannot be overlooked. The degree to which we forgive is the exact degree of forgiveness for which we ask. Do we not reap what we sow?

...Lead us not into temptation, but deliver us from evil...

To complete the trifold time supplication, an entreaty for deliverance from sin and separation, in the **future**, we ask for us to be led. This active leading implies a continual and moving aspect to our spiritual growth, away from temptation, to become kingdom seekers.

This prayer praises God and asks for the kingdom of God and of heaven to come to us in all that we do and in all times – past, present, and future. We then ask for "peace in our day" and to be "free of anxiety, waiting in joyful hope" for Christ's coming again. But more importantly, we ask this for everyone. We do not once speak in the first person.

Three times throughout the day – at Mass, during Evening prayer, and during Morning Prayer – the Church asks us to pray this prayer. Let it be prayed, but more importantly, let it be lived.

Both now and forever.

26

THE SIGN OF PEACE

"Lord Jesus Christ, you said to your apostles, I leave you peace, my peace I give to you. Look not on our sins, but on the faith of your church, and grant us peace and unity of your kingdom, where you live forever and ever."

The church expresses that this sign of peace is an outward expression of "mutual charity" and "ecclesial communion" with each other before receiving the sacrament. Mutual charity needs no explanation. Charity is given and received, and by this we express our communion with one another. Do you see the similarities between the words communion and community? The Eucharist reveals a profound dimension of itself: Christ in each other.

When we make the sign of peace at Mass, we offer peace to so much more than the people around us. Though logistically it would be impossible to offer a material expression of peace to everyone around in church that day, in reality, this is what we do. When we look into the eyes of the person next to us, or behind us, and shake hands, smile and nod, or embrace, we offer this to everyone. We offer peace with that person to be sure, but I would venture that this person also becomes a representation, or stand-in, for everyone with whom we offer peace. If we are sincere in our offering of true Christian peace, we would be aware that to offer peace to one is to offer peace to all. Who would Jesus exclude from peace? Precisely…

When we say 'peace be with you', we are perhaps in our most non-discriminatory state. The *you* we speak of is both second person singular and second person plural. If we want peace and unity in the kingdom, how can we justify withholding our peace from anyone? Again, could you imagine Christ offering peace to some and choosing to keep peace from others? If we keep true to the spirit of the Liturgy, our offered peace extends far beyond us.

Just prior to this time, we prayed for peace to be granted to "our day" in the Lord's Prayer. Now we offer this visible, material sign of peace. But deeper still, we offer a visible sign of our commitment to peace beyond this particular moment to our Monday-through-Saturday moments. At the end of the Mass, we will be told to 'go in peace'. This just confirms the commitment we have made to the sign of peace.

A final observation… Is it any coincidence that when warring parties make peace they 'come to the table' and when we receive communion we come to the table (altar) of the Lord? Is it any wonder that Christ is the 'Prince of Peace'?

Peace be with you.

27

THE FRACTION RITE

Of the fraction rite, the Church, in its instruction contained in the *Roman Missal*, states the following:

> "The priest breaks the Eucharistic Bread...[this] gesture of breaking bread at the Last Supper, signifies that the many faithful are made one body (1 Cor 10:17) by receiving Communion from the one Bread of Life which is Christ, who died and rose for the salvation of the world. The priest breaks the Bread and puts a piece of the host into the chalice to signify the unity of the Body and Blood of the Lord in the work of salvation, namely, of the living and glorious Body of Jesus Christ."

While this is done, the *Agnus Dei*, or Lamb of God, is

sung in a three-fold supplication for mercy and peace. The Trinitarian parallel is no accident.

The Father offers the sacrifice of his Son, who in turn sends the Holy Spirit to carry out and continue our call to oneness in Christ's salvation.

Why have we continued to be moved by a crucified Christ dying to rise so that we might die and rise? There's a reason that paradoxes resonate and speak so profoundly to our nature's inner sense of truth-seeking. The paradox of a brokenness that bespeaks restoration of wholeness not only reflects a profound Paschal, Christian reality, but offers a sense of hope in the resurrection. In dying, we will rise anew. Throughout this Liturgy, we see unity dominating — thematically speaking — and division disintegrating into profound unity and peace. What have we been doing for unity?

The lamb, an historical object of sacrifice, takes away all sin and saves a lost world, lighting a path that had been filled with darkness. The idea that from as 'insignificant' of an animal as a lamb can bring about earthly salvation truly brings to focus the profundity of 'the least of these', and the 'last shall be first'. Further, to ask for mercy from someone so often referred to as an insignificant lamb bridges the gap between the last and least so as to render opposites not only insignificant, but non-existent. This non-existence becomes a realm of the infinite, a realm reserved for that of the divine kingdom, and a granting of peace.

A body sacrificed – broken for us all – brings about unity. This is a true hallmark of the kingdom. It is a kingdom of peace, and granted unto us when we all partake in this communion with Christ (i.e., reception of Christ) and become one.

For the sake of the peace that we sing ought to be

granted to us, how much longer can we tolerate division? Christ was beaten, humiliated, and died because he thought differently than those around him – indeed, was different – so that he might inspire unity among us. If we are not actively working to eradicate division and differences through dialogue and prayer, what does that say about our willingness to bring about the peace we desire to be granted unto us?

"Lord, I am not worthy that you should enter under my roof, but only say the word and I shall be healed." Being healed implies a restoration to wholeness. We're not worthy, because we insist on living in division.

Are we ready for healing?

28

THE COMMUNION PROCESSION

We have come to the summit of the Liturgy of the Eucharist, and the pinnacle of the Mass itself: the reception of Holy Communion. Let us consider the sublime reality of this moment, which I posit is the very reason we come to Mass in the first place, and likely why we continue.

First, we experience the procession to the altar. In a very orderly fashion, we exit our pews and we fall into a line of people. We are, at the same time, individual and non-individual, as we become part of something much bigger. Our conscious decision to walk into line displays an act of faith. It demonstrates to us that when we said, *"only say the word and I shall be healed,"* we believed that to be true. We believe that He has said the word, having spoken on our behalf by his death. Is it any accident that during communion we have an image of hundreds of people walking toward the crucifix, approaching our own brokenness? So many people wanting and needing to be healed, and realizing together who the Divine Physician is. Our contrition compels us.

Next, we have the time it takes for us to walk down the aisle to receive. What do we do with this time? What does this time represent? It's so personal yet to so communal at the same time. What goes on in our minds? Our walk culminates everything that came before and at the same time orients us for everything yet to come. It constitutes an integral element of the Liturgy. No one can make this walk for us, and yet we are comforted in knowing that we all walk it together.

Then, there is the moment of reception… the Body of Christ. Four words, so simply said, yet so complex in its meaning. It means that though we receive something so ordinary feeling, looking, and tasting, it truly is in essence the Body of Christ. Further, it affirms our membership in the Body of Christ. Our 'amen' both publicly and privately states this belief. And just as Christ walked to Calvary and died, we walk to communion and commit to our own death of self so that Christ may dwell in us. As the Body dissolves and disappears into us, our 'selves' dissolve and disappear into Christ. If there is doubt in this presence, step into faith and allow Christ to happen.

If we decide to take the Blood of Christ, again, we taste ordinary wine, but know that it is something bigger – Christ's presence. What does this say about the ordinary in life? I lament the day when ordinary became an unconsciously accepted concept, and dream of a day when all of life will be what we call extraordinary.

After this, when we have returned to our seat in the pews, there is some time spent in prayer before the priest concludes with the *Prayer after Communion*, praying for what has already begun – the fruition of this rite – that our oneness in Christ continues to be lived in the world. How blessed we are to take part in this Eucharist, and have Jesus Christ now dwelling within us, wanting to be taken out into our lives to further his work on earth, and bring forth the kingdom. It's no wonder people leave Mass right after communion! Obviously, they simply just can't wait to spread the Good News!!

May the Body of Christ bring us to everlasting life.

29

THE FINAL BLESSING

It is after the post-communion prayer and before the final blessing that the Church allows for any necessary announcements. This is why announcements are done at this time. But what do announcements have to do with Mass, and why are they allowed in the first place? If we think of the Mass as fostering unity among Christians and continuing the work of spreading the kingdom, we can see how every announcement, if deemed necessary enough to announce, directly relates to doing the work of Christ in a very real and community-fostering sense. Listen for this connection.

After this, we have the final blessing, of which there are three forms. It is at the discretion of the priest which one is used. They are:

1) A simple form
2) A solemn blessing
3) A prayer over the people

The first form, the simplest of the three, blesses all of us in the name of the Father, Son, and Holy Spirit, giving us the commission to allow the Trinity to be lived through us as we go out into the world.

The second form, the solemn blessing, is employed during solemnities and special seasons of the Church year. It elevates the solemnity of the occasion and thematically relates to the season or day being celebrated. In bowing our heads for God's blessing, the priest asks a series of petitions on our behalf, to which we respond, "*Amen.*" For example, the solemn blessing for All Saints asks that the saints' examples of holy living may turn our thoughts to service of both God and neighbor.

The third option for the final blessing is the prayer over the people. This form may be used at the discretion of the priest. For example, the prayer over the people during the feast day of a saint may ask that we have fellowship with the saint and unending joy in the kingdom.

Is it necessary to stay for this blessing? I think that's the wrong question to ask, so I offer no answer. Should you want to stay for this blessing? Again, if we approach it with the idea of 'should' we get pulled back to issues of necessity versus nonessential and I'm not sure that's a healthy approach to maturing spirituality. Put simply, do you *want* to stay for this blessing? Do you feel compelled to stay for this blessing? Where is the source of that compulsion?

In the beginning of this book, we spoke of Christ's original and personal invitation to us to enter the upper room and to do this in memory of Him. After the Last Supper, Christ was crucified and died. The apostles probably wanted every moment they could have with Him. The final blessing at Mass, during which we remember his sacrifice, is one more 'final moment' that we are afforded to experience His presence in community. Do we not crave for one more moment with those we love when they are dying? With the final blessing, we are given 'another moment' with Him who died for all, and His very real presence, standing among a community that has just received Him in the Eucharist. What a blessed opportunity! How blessed are we?!

30

THE DISMISSAL

And about an hour or so after the beginning of Mass, we have reached the dismissal. The new translation of the *Roman Missal*, in use since Advent 2011, slightly changes the familiar dismissal of, "*Go in the peace of Christ to love and serve the Lord.*" Our response of "*thanks be to God*" remains the same, but we are commissioned by the following words, (of which there will are four options):

1)   *Go forth, the Mass is ended.*
2)   *Go and announce the Gospel of the Lord.*
3)   *Go in peace, glorifying the Lord by your life.*
4)   *Go in peace.*

Each is slightly different, with unique characteristics. The first option is a simple statement of the Mass's temporal finality. The second announces a command, while the third has a directive of glorifying. The last simply invites us to a disposition of peace. Though varied, the shared, common theme is the definitive directive to "*go*." (It's kinder and more filled with meaning than, "Get out.") The going forth, whether we then announce, glorify, or simply leave in a state of peace, is an active command. We are not to go passively. We go with homework, or life work, as it were. The Mass as an event in time may have ended, but our mission, through our baptism, continues outside of the church doors.

It is worthwhile to note that the part of announcing that we are to go in peace properly belongs to the deacon, who is ordained in a life of charity, good works, and preaching the gospel. When he announces this to us, it is as if we are ordained to the same work, each charged with our own corners of the world, letting the gospel of Christ be announced through our words and, more importantly, through our lives. And when our lives announce the Gospel, what a wondrous glorification of God this is!

The sacrifice, the Mass, has ended. However, Christ's death was not the end, but rather the beginning of the mission to bring about the kingdom. So then we go forth. We continue glorifying and announcing. And when we do this, we bring peace. The now unspoken '*to love and serve the Lord*' part, though no longer spoken, is no less understood as a given. I'm reminded of Saint Francis, that 12th century champion of peace, who said to preach the gospel always, and when necessary, use words.

Go in peace.

31

THE RECESSIONAL HYMN

We've been told to go forth in peace; to announce and to glorify. We carry the gospel out in our hearts, and sing of His peace. Though they are arguably not a specific component of the Liturgy, postludes and recessional hymns have become commonplace.

When I moved to Arizona a few years ago, the college choir I had been directing gave me a pocket watch with the inscription *"May your heart never be without song"* as a departing gift. I've never forgotten this, and make a conscious effort to live such that there is always song within me. Biased as I readily admit to being (as a music minister), I cannot imagine life without song.

I think, for me, the definitions and conceptions that have evolved over the years, especially since being involved in Liturgy, are those of '*sing*' and '*song*'. At the beginning of this book, I used the same phrase that the church uses for the Mass: "*A perfect song of praise and thanksgiving.*" (How appropriate for Eucharist, which means thanksgiving!) Singing, strictly speaking, is a vocal utterance – drawn out speech to produce a melodic sound. But this definition leaves quite a bit to be desired. To sing must presume that there is something to be sung, namely, a song.

A song in the literal sense can be thought of as a collection of words and organized pitches and notes. Before this, though, there was something ephemeral, ineffable, almost mystical (…perhaps a sense of some truth that was felt…), and the song was just the material expression of what already is and has been. (And will be.) In this sense, the song has always been, for it points to and expresses an eternal truth. In the recessional hymn, this truth was lived in the person of Christ, and sung by his life and sacrifice – a song of praise and thanksgiving to the Father.

In the opening of the gospel of John we read: "In the beginning was the Word." I'd like to believe that in the beginning was, indeed, the Word, and that it was sung. We were sung into being, and when we sing of Christ, we sing Him into being. When this happens, what a beautiful song we hear! Can you imagine what that might sound like?

When I moved Arizona, it was a new adventure and a new beginning, and looking back I feel that the college choir I directed knew exactly what I needed to hear. Perhaps as we leave Mass in peace, the same advice should apply…

May your heart never be without (His) song.

32

REMEMBERING OUR BAPTISM

Our fingers dip into the stoups of holy water as we exit the church and go out into the world. With a few drops, we cross ourselves in the name of the Father, Son, and the Holy Spirit, and remind ourselves of our own baptism. It is no coincidence that in the Rite of Baptism, we hear of Christ asking of us to *"Go out and teach all nations, baptizing them in the name of the Father, Son, and Holy Spirit."* This is the call of which the Mass reminds us. Recently, I read of a church abandoning the practice of a parish council debating and word-sculpting to create a perfect mission statement to print on their bulletin. The church simply adopted that quote from Matthew 28:19. How brilliant, I thought.

Reminded of our baptism and our calling by this water, we affirm our being blessed, and now live as a blessed people. Imagine if every day we began recognizing that blessings are being poured upon us. The classic cinematic image of looking up with arms outstretched, eyes closed to more fully sense the joy, laughing uproariously as rain showers down upon us comes to mind. Christ himself showed us on the cross to live our lives with our arms outstretched and opened, ready to love.

Gene Kelly sang in *"Singin' in the Rain"*: *"The sun's in my heart, I'm ready for love."* As we leave Mass, the Son is indeed in our hearts, and once again we are ready to love, as torrents of blessings rain upon us. Let us therefore go out and teach all people that it's okay to come out and get soaked.

33

EPILOGUE: THE WORK OF THE PEOPLE

When my niece, Anna, was about six months old, my sister, who lives in St. Louis, called me to tell me that Anna was seated upon her bed and planted her little feet on the mattress, grabbed hold of the laundry basket and pulled her little self up. She looked at my sister's beaming face and just giggled. I got a bit choked up at the joy in her voice when she told me this, and I just imagine the precious look that she must have shared when little Anna giggled.

What does this have to do with the Liturgy? Perhaps nothing, but then again, I think it has everything to do with Liturgy. Liturgy as we mentioned in the beginning of this book is 'work of the people' for the sanctification of people and for the glory of God; the most perfect song of praise and thanksgiving to God. Bear with me as I try to relate the two.

When we come Sunday after Sunday, like little Anna, we

plant our fragile feet in the comfort of God's mercy and compassion. Through the infinite cross and Christ's dying and rising we are able to grab onto the laundry basket, which becomes the communal support of each other and the rock and surety that is God's unconditional love. We struggle, tirelessly pull, confess our desire to be better, hear God's voice and find God in the blessedness of each other. In other words, we experience Mass.

When we pull our fragile and unsure selves up and find our footing in God's compassion, we receive the Lord. And just like Anna's giggle when she pulled herself up and met my sister's face, our hearts also overflow with joy when we come face to face with God in the Eucharist. Imagine the joy in God's face when we stand there, having pulled ourselves up from our sinfulness, with each other's undiscriminating help and God's infinite grace. Imagine the moment we become completely enraptured with Him, and that child within that truly has never grown up, giggles with complete abandon with God. That sound, I believe, would be quite the song of thanksgiving.

May we continue the work of the people.

ABOUT THE AUTHORS

Adam Thomé is a freelance writer living in Arizona. Growing up in a traditionally-minded Catholic family and environment, as well as attending Catholic school through high school, Adam's spiritual foundation is decidedly Catholic. Growing in awareness of the social issues of our times as well as the teachings of Christ on the treatment of the poor and marginalized, Adam began to feel a great disconnect from the church he called home and its hierarchical priorities. Always keeping one foot in the door with his love and attraction to the Liturgy, Adam found hope in finding that a seeming majority of Catholics also felt the Catholic views of social teachings need to be revisited, openly discussed, and ultimately evolve to resonate with the life and teaching of Christ. Adam can be reached at adam@catholicmajority.com.

Tim Ferreira is a professional in the developmental disabilities field who happens to also have a passion for Catholicism. The son of an ordained Roman Catholic deacon, Tim attended Catholic schools from kindergarten through high school, and spent a good portion of his formative years in and around the Church on both the East and West coasts of the United States. After high school, Tim fell away from the faith, feeling increasingly estranged from the Catholic hierarchy and teachings on contemporary social issues. In the past ten years, Tim has felt increasingly drawn back into the faith and is particularly interested in supporting the voices of Catholics who feel that their voices are being drowned out by an increasingly vocal, traditionalist minority who represent the Church to the media. He has a BA in philosophy from North Carolina State University, a certificate in Nonprofit Management from Duke University, and is currently working on a M.Ed. in Adult Education. Tim currently lives in North Carolina with his partner and a small menagerie of domestic animals. Tim may be contacted at tim@catholicmajority.com

COPYRIGHT

FIRST EDITION
ISBN 978-0-9912311-0-2

ABOUT THE PUBLISHER

Catholic Majority is the website for Catholics who feel marginalized on other Catholic sites. Visit us online at http://catholicmajority.com! Follow us on Facebook or Twitter for periodic updates about our activities and future publications. Feel free to contact us anytime at contact@catholicmajority.com.

Who We Are: We are men and women of conscience who value the contributions of the Catholic Church, identify as Roman Catholics, and who wish to offer an alternative to the viewpoints espoused by the vocal minority of Catholics whose "expertise" is often sought after by the media. Catholic Majority seeks to bring an honest and nuanced voice to the table and provide an alternative narrative that represents Catholicism to the public and to the world. We believe that the majority of Catholics value diversity, and that the voice of the Catholic majority deserves to be heard as much as that of the minority.

Our Mission: We are committed to providing a voice for the diversity within the Mystical Body of Christ, with respect, for the betterment of the Church.

Our Vision: We contribute to the unity of Christ's Body by embracing diversity in accordance with the Catechism of the Catholic Church, section 791, which states: "The body's unity does not do away with the diversity of its members...[It] produces and stimulates charity among the faithful...[and] triumphs over all human divisions."

Our Values: We believe, along with the Catechism, that "conscience is man's most secret core, and his sanctuary. There he is alone with God whose voice echoes in his depths" (section 1795). Accordingly, we agree with section 1789, that: "Some rules apply in every case: One must never do evil so that good may result from it; the Golden Rule: 'Whatever you wish that men would do to you, do so to them'; [and] charity always proceeds by way of respect for one's neighbor and his conscience: 'Thus sinning against your brethren and wounding their conscience...you sin against Christ.' Therefore 'it is right not to...do anything that makes your brother stumble.'"

Made in the USA
Lexington, KY
30 December 2013